DETROIT PUBLIC LIBRARY

3 5674 00434152 6

W9-CJR-048

DETROIT PUBLIC LIBRARY

PLEASE RETURN TO KNAPP BRANCH LIBRARY
13330 CONANT   DETROIT, MI 48212
876-0133

DATE DUE

APR 25 1994

NOV 0 9 1996

Visual Geography Series®

AUSTRALIA

...in Pictures

Prepared by
Geography Department

Lerner Publications Company
Minneapolis

Copyright © 1990 by Lerner Publications Compan

All rights reserved. International copyright secure
No part of this book may be reproduced, stored in
retrieval system, or transmitted in any form or by any
means—electronic, mechanical, photocopying, record-
ing, or otherwise—without the prior written permis-
sion of the publisher, except for the inclusion of brief
quotations in an acknowledged review.

Harry Jonas Lerner
Associate Publisher
Nancy M. Campbell
Senior Editor
Mary M. Rodgers
Editors
Gretchen Bratvold
Dan Filbin
Phyllis Schuster
Photo Researchers
Karen A. Sirvaitis
Kerstin Coyle
Editorial/Photo Assistant
Marybeth Campbell
Consultants/Contributors
Ward Barrett
Sandra K. Davis
Designer
Jim Simondet
Cartographer
Carol F. Barrett
Indexers
Kristine S. Schubert
Sylvia Timian
Production Manager
Gary J. Hansen

Photo by Sue Guernsey

A cemetery on Tasmania contains the graves of convicts who died while confined in the island's Port Arthur prison.

This book is an all-new edition in the Visual Geography Series. Previous editions were published by
Sterling Publishing Company, New York City. The
text, set in 10/12 Century Textbook, is fully revised
and updated, and new photographs, maps, charts, and
captions have been added.

LIBRARY OF CONGRESS CATALOGING-IN-PUBLICATION DATA

Australia in pictures / prepared by Geography Depart-
ment, Lerner Publications Company.
   p.   cm. – (Visual geography series)
   Rev. ed. of: Australia in pictures / prepared by Jo
McDonald and Reven Uihlein.
   Includes bibliographical references.
   Summary: An introduction to the land, history, gov-
ernment, economy, people, and culture of Australia.
   ISBN 0-8225-1855-4
   1. Australia. [1. Australia.] I. McDonald, Jo. Aus-
tralia in pictures. II. Lerner Publications Company.
Geography Dept. III. Series: Visual geography series
(Minneapolis, Minn.)
DU96.A964   1990
994—dc20   89-29199
                                     CIP
                                      AC

International Standard Book Number: 0-8225-1855-4
Library of Congress Catalog Card Number: 89-29199

Courtesy of Australian Information Service

Children in remote parts of Australia attend the School of the Air, using a radio to talk with distant teachers.

Acknowledgements

Title page photo by Tourism Australia.

Elevation contours adapted from *The Times Atlas of
the World*, seventh comprehensive edition (New York:
Times Books, 1985).

Photo by Sandi and Jim Provencher

Signs on the Boomerang Sandwich Bar in suburban Sydney reflect Australia's ties to two diverse cultures—the Aboriginal and the British. A boomerang is a hunting weapon that Aborigines developed thousands of years ago. Food items offered on the small sign—fish, chips, and bacon and egg rolls—are British snacks that are popular in Britain's former colonies.

Contents

INDONESIA

ARAFURA SEA

TIMOR
SEA

PAPUA
NEW
GUINEA

INDIAN OCEAN

Darwin
Batchelor
KAKADU
NAT. PK.
S. Alligator R.

Daly R.

CAPE
YORK
PEN.

Gulf of
Carpentaria

CORAL SEA

GREEN I.

Fitzroy R.

Broome

NORTHWEST
SHELF

Port
Hedlund

NORTHERN   TERRITORY

Mitchell R.

Flinders R.

GREAT BARRIER REEF

WESTERN AUSTRALIA

ULURU
NAT. PK.

Alice Springs

QUEENSLAND

Fitzroy R.

Dawson R.

HERON I.

Murchison R.

SOUTH AUSTRALIA

Lake Eyre

Brisbane R.

Noosa

Brisbane

Coober Pedy

Lake
Torrens

Lake
Frome

Darling R.

NEW SOUTH WALES

Kalgoorlie

Lake
Gairdner

Broken
Hill

Gulgong

Swan R.

Perth

GREAT AUSTRALIAN
BIGHT

Port Lincoln

Port
Adelaide

Adelaide

Murray R.

Lachlan R.

Griffith
Murrumbidgee R.

Bathurst

Sydney
Botany Bay

TERR. OF JERVIS BAY

VICTORIA

Goulburn R.

Cabramurra
Thredbo

CANBERRA
AUST. CAP. TERR.

Melbourne

Yarra R.

Bass Strait

TASMAN SEA

TASMANIA

Derwent R.

TASMAN PENINSULA
Port Arthur

Hobart

N
↑

AUSTRALIA

State and Territory Boundaries

Major Roads

0   200   400 Miles

0   200   400 Kilometers

OCEANIA
AUSTRALIA

0   1000 Miles
0   1000 Kilometers

120°

150°

Equator

0°

PACIFIC   OCEAN

Tropic of Capricorn

30°

30°

TASMAN SEA

120°

150°

180°

METRIC CONVERSION CHART
To Find Approximate Equivalents

WHEN YOU KNOW:	MULTIPLY BY:	TO FIND:
AREA		
acres	0.41	hectares
square miles	2.59	square kilometers
CAPACITY		
gallons	3.79	liters
LENGTH		
feet	30.48	centimeters
yards	0.91	meters
miles	1.61	kilometers
MASS (weight)		
pounds	0.45	kilograms
tons	0.91	metric tons
VOLUME		
cubic yards	0.77	cubic meters
TEMPERATURE		
degrees Fahrenheit	0.56 (*after* subtracting 32)	degrees Celsius

Photo by Chris Fairclough

These Aboriginal children—descendants of Australia's earliest inhabitants—live in the Northern Territory. Their parents work on a cattle ranch. Most Aborigines have a lower standard of living than that of white Australians.

Introduction

Australia, a large country in the South Pacific Ocean, occupies the world's smallest and flattest continent. In this remote land, unusual animals evolved. At least 40,000 years ago, the Aborigines—Australia's first people—began to arrive. As centuries passed, more than 500 Aboriginal groups developed, each occupying a separate territory. A complex religion and strong patterns of social conduct governed the Aborigines' lives.

Hundreds of generations of Aborigines lived undisturbed by foreign influences until the late 1700s, when Great Britain claimed Australia as its territory. Britain wanted a place to which it could send criminals, and Australia met that need. As their familiarity with the remote continent increased, however, the British came to recognize Australia's economic potential. Settlers pushed Aborigines off the best land, and Australia began to develop as a European outpost in the South Pacific.

Eventually, six British colonies formed in Australia, and they often engaged in rivalry, rather than cooperation. In the late 1800s, the colonial governments decided unity would help them solve their common problems. The country peacefully gained its independence in 1901 and continued to maintain close political and commercial ties with Britain.

By the 1950s, Australians enjoyed a high standard of living. Discoveries of large mineral deposits and energy resources added to the country's prosperity. As mining and manufacturing grew, labor shortages developed. The government encouraged immigration to provide more workers for industry.

As Europeans, Asians, and Americans arrived in large numbers, the population took on greater ethnic diversity. In time, Australians also became more responsive to the rights and needs of the Aborigines, whose way of life had been disrupted when Europeans moved in.

In the 1970s, changes in European trading patterns and a fall in world demand for Australia's products hurt the nation's economy. Frequent labor strikes added to the country's difficulties. High unemployment and inflation continued to be problems in the 1980s. Yet by the end of that decade Australia's efforts to improve the economy had met with some success.

Courtesy of Richard Southward

After a music class, students in Griffith, New South Wales, wash their recorders at a drinking fountain in the school yard.

Photo by Sandi and Jim Provencher

Jutting rocks mark hillsides near Australia's highest peak, Mount Kosciusko, situated in southeastern Australia.

1) The Land

Australia is the only nation in the world to occupy a whole continent. The country, which lies entirely within the Southern Hemisphere, is 2,000 miles southeast of mainland Asia. Its territory of almost three million square miles is about the same size as the United States without Alaska. In area, Australia ranks as the sixth largest country in the world.

At its greatest distances, Australia stretches 1,950 miles north to south and 2,475 miles west to east. The mainland contains five of Australia's six states—namely, Queensland, New South Wales, Victoria, South Australia, and Western Australia. The continent also includes the Northern Territory, a largely barren region that occupies almost one-fifth of the land area. Tasmania, an island southeast of the mainland, is the sixth Australian state.

With inlets included, Australia's shoreline is about 22,800 miles long. North of the mainland, from west to east, are the Timor, Arafura, and Coral seas. The South Pacific Ocean and the Tasman Sea lie to the east, and the Indian Ocean touches the country's southern and western shores. Bass Strait separates Tasmania from the mainland, leading westward to the Great Australian Bight—a 600-mile-wide bay on the continent's southern coast. The 400-mile-wide Gulf of Carpentaria indents the continent's northern edge.

Topography

Australia has three distinct geographic regions—the Great Western Plateau, the Central Lowlands, and the Eastern Highlands. The Great Western Plateau occupies

7

Australians call the heart of their country the Red Centre after the color of the soil. Dry shrubs are typical of the vegetation.

Photo by Sue Guernsey

the western three-fifths of Australia. Most of the plateau is outback—the term Australians use for dry, sparsely inhabited interior parts of the continent. The Eastern Highlands form a band down Australia's eastern coast. Separating the western and eastern regions are the Central Lowlands, which lie above a vast reserve of underground water called the Great Artesian Basin.

Within the Great Western Plateau lie the entire state of Western Australia, much of the Northern Territory, a great part of South Australia, and a portion of western Queensland. Very flat overall, the region has an average elevation of 1,000 feet above sea level. In its center are three deserts—the Great Sandy, the Gibson, and the Great Victoria. The Great Sandy and Great Victoria deserts are areas of swirl-

Courtesy of Australian Tourist Commission

The Olgas—28 massive boulders in Uluru National Park—rise near the continent's geographic center. These formations and Ayers Rock, 20 miles away, attract many tourists.

8

ing sands and giant dunes. To the north and southwest of the deserts are hilly scrublands that can support livestock.

The wettest and most fertile sections of the Great Western Plateau are the coastal plains in the far north and in the southwest. A 400-mile-long treeless plateau called the Nullarbor Plain extends along the southern edge of the plateau north of the Great Australian Bight.

The Central Lowlands cover much of Queensland and New South Wales and parts of Victoria and South Australia. Except for the coastal sections in the north and south, the lowlands are too dry and hot for crop farming. Inland riverbeds are empty most of the year. The region supports a sheep industry, however, due to the Great Artesian Basin, from which wells draw water for livestock. The barren Simpson Desert forms the west central part of the lowlands. At the southern edge of this desert is Lake Eyre, which at 52 feet below sea level is the lowest point in Australia.

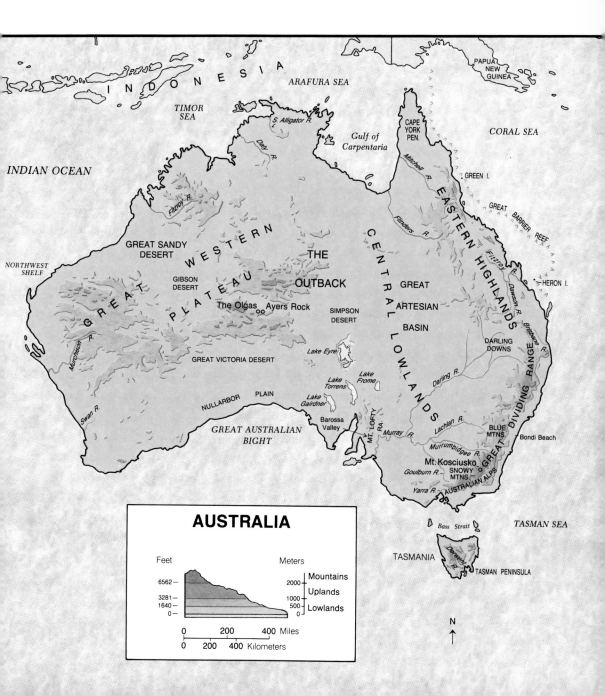

AUSTRALIA

Courtesy of Australian Information Service

A snow gum (eucalyptus) tree grows near Cabramurra in the Snowy Mountains of the Australian Alps.

Courtesy of Tourism Australia

Using poles to steady themselves, reef walkers on Heron Island study the aquatic life of the Great Barrier Reef.

The Eastern Highlands, also called the Great Dividing Range, extend from Cape York Peninsula in the northeast to the southern coast of Tasmania. The coastal areas of Queensland and New South Wales, much of Victoria, and the island of Tasmania lie in the Eastern Highlands. This region of low mountains, plateaus, and coastal plains contains some fertile soil and receives more rain than the rest of the country does. Most Australians live in the southern half of this area.

The highest elevations in Australia are in the extreme southern part of the Eastern Highlands. Mount Kosciusko (7,310 feet)—the country's tallest peak—rises from the Australian Alps in the southeastern corner of the continent. Across Bass Strait, mountains also dominate the island of Tasmania. Formerly called Van Diemen's Land, this state contains several peaks that exceed 4,000 feet.

The Great Barrier Reef, the largest deposit of coral in the world, stretches for 1,250 miles along the northeastern coast of Australia. An underwater wall that is home to many rare forms of sea life, the Great Barrier Reef is actually a chain of 2,600 coral reefs and 320 coral islands. In the north, the reef lies close to the mainland. It gradually spreads outward, and the southern tip is 150 miles from the continent.

Water Resources

Major underground basins that collect and store water lie beneath 60 percent of Australia's land surface. People and livestock in interior regions rely on wells that tap these stores of groundwater. The greatest reserves are in the Great Artesian Basin. Much of the water in this basin is salty, however, and can be drunk only by livestock.

The 1,600-mile-long Murray River and its tributaries—the Darling, Murrumbidgee, Lachlan, and Goulburn rivers—form the country's largest river system. This net-

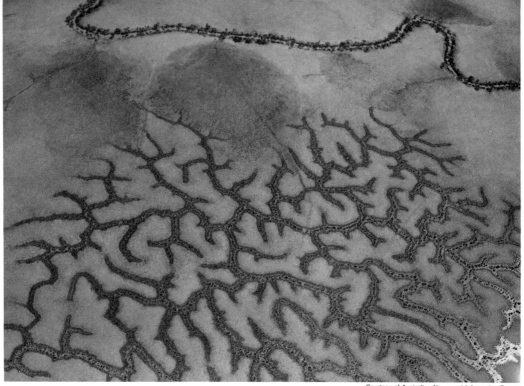

Courtesy of Australian News and Information Bureau

Summer rains flood the plains of "Channel Country," a 300,000-square-mile area in southwestern Queensland and adjoining parts of South Australia. The grasses that grow after the waters recede make this part of the Central Lowlands the best cattle-fattening country in Australia. Coolabah and red gum trees line the main water courses.

work of waterways extends over a large part of southeastern Australia. These rivers supply 80 percent of Australia's irrigated land with water.

The Snowy Mountains Scheme, which was completed in 1974, is a massive water-conservation and hydroelectric project. Aqueducts (canals) and tunnels collect the flow from melting snows in the Snowy Mountains—a range in the Australian Alps. These channels carry the runoff to dams and reservoirs for use during dry periods. Other tunnels redirect mountain streams that formerly ran eastward into the Tasman Sea. Rerouted to the Murray and Murrumbidgee rivers, this additional fresh water increases the ability of these rivers to irrigate southeastern Australia.

Lake Eyre, situated in the outback of South Australia, is the country's largest lake. Because of infrequent rains, however, this desert lake's floor—called a playa—is usually dry. Floods have allowed the huge salt lake to reach its full size only twice since Europeans began keeping records about the surrounding desert. Other large playas in South Australia form Lake Torrens, Lake Gairdner, and Lake Frome.

Climate

A hot, tropical climate marks most of northern Australia. The southern half of the continent is in the temperate zone. Because Australia lies in the Southern Hemisphere, summer occurs from December to February, and the winter months are June, July, and August.

In the north, the average temperature is 84° F in January (the hottest month for most of the country) and 77° F in July. In the south, those same months bring average readings of 63° and 46° F. Some parts of interior Australia, however, see average daily highs above 100° F in January. When summer winds blow from the interior, the cities on the eastern coast get very warm.

Winters can be chilly in the south, and mountain ranges there receive considerable amounts of snow. The coldest regions of Australia are the highlands of Tasmania and the southeastern corner of the continent. In central Australia, winter brings cool nights, but the days are usually warm and dry.

Australia receives the least rainfall of any inhabited continent. Most of the country's riverbeds are dry for at least part of the year, filling only during the rainy season. In northern Australia, the wet period occurs during the summer, from December to February. In the south, rain falls primarily in the winter, from June to August. Moisture evaporates rapidly throughout much of the continent, but floods are common in important agricultural areas.

Flora and Fauna

Because it is isolated from other large landmasses, Australia has plants and an-

Courtesy of Australian Tourist Commission

Winters usually bring heavy snowfalls to the Snowy Mountains, which are a favorite destination for skiers.

Photo by Emily Slowinski

Magnolia and wattle (acacia) trees bloom near the Maritime Museum in Hobart, Tasmania. The yellow wattle is Australia's unofficial floral emblem. Wattles can survive in the dry scrublands of the outback (dry, interior regions).

Photo by John Clifton

The red kangaroo can hop 40 miles an hour and can jump as high as 20 feet.

imals that can be found nowhere else in the world. Low rainfall levels encourage vegetation that can withstand drought. Tough, spiny leaves and thick bark hold moisture in plants and increase their resistance to fire—a seasonal danger except in rainy coastal areas.

Australia's best-known trees—the gum (also called eucalyptus) and the wattle (acacia)—grow in all regions of the country except the driest deserts. Of the 550 species of gum trees, the jarrah is prized for its extremely hard and durable wood. More than 600 types of wattle—a flowering tree—can be found throughout the country. The yellow wattle appears on the Australian coat of arms.

More than half of Australia's 230 species of native mammals are marsupials—animals that develop their young in a pouch. This group includes koalas, Tasmanian devils, possums, wombats, bandicoots, and 45 species of kangaroos. The tree-dwelling koala feeds on gum leaves, which

Courtesy of Ruth Karl

Colonies of blue coral grow near Green Island in the Great Barrier Reef. Individual coral animals, called polyps, are less than five-sixteenths of an inch in diameter. Living colonies contain millions of polyps that cover structures of dead coral.

have a high oil content. The oil enables the animal to go without water for long periods of time. Although the meat-eating Tasmanian devil is only the size of a small dog, it is strong enough to kill a sheep. The wombat is a burrowing marsupial found only in Australia.

Some mammals that are native to Australia and New Guinea are unusual because they lay eggs. Called monotremes, these species include the echidna (spiny anteater) and the duck-billed platypus. One of Australia's most powerful predators is the dingo, or wild dog. The first

Independent Picture Service

Australia's unique animals include the Tasmanian devil *(left)*, the koala *(lower left)*—both marsupials—and the dingo *(lower right).* Disease and the destruction of their native habitats threaten the survival of koalas, whose population has been reduced to about 400,000.

Independent Picture Service

Independent Picture Service

Independent Picture Service

Monotremes are unusual mammals that lay eggs but nurse their young. Only two types of monotremes still exist—the platypus *(above)* and the echidna *(right)*—and both can be found in Australia. The fur-coated, duckbilled platypus uses its tail like a rudder while swimming. A short-legged variety of the echidna, also known as the spiny anteater, lives on the Australian mainland.

Independent Picture Service

dingoes probably came to the continent from Asia with Aborigines thousands of years ago.

At least 700 species of birds are native to Australia. Among them are black swans, flightless giant emus, and about 60 kinds of parrots—including cockatoos and parakeets. Many Australian birds are noted for unusual songs and behaviors. The lyrebird—named because the shape of its tail resembles the ancient stringed instrument—can mimic the songs of other creatures. The male bowerbird builds bowers, or arched shelters, in which it performs elaborate courtship dances to attract females. The kookaburra's call sounds like human laughter ringing through the forests.

Natural Resources

Australia contains rich deposits of many metals and minerals. Its supply of iron ore

South Australia contains most of Australia's and the world's opals. The opal-mining industry, which provides jobs for about 4,000 people, is centered in Coober Pedy, a town whose Aboriginal name means "man in hole." Temperatures there reach 120° F in summer. To escape from the heat, residents live in underground houses.

Courtesy of Australian Tourist Commission

ranks among the largest in the world. The country is also a major producer of bauxite—the principal source of aluminum. Great reserves of coal and uranium exist in Australia, and supplies of natural gas and crude oil have been developed.

Australia is a major supplier of lead, zinc, copper, and nickel, as well as an important source of mineral sands used to make heavy metals. The country also contains tin, silver, and some precious gems, including diamonds and opals. Gold—the metal that touched off massive immigration to Australia in 1851—is still mined in Western Australia and Queensland.

Major Urban Centers

Despite its large size and low population density, Australia is a very urbanized country. Less than 15 percent of its 16.8 million people live in rural areas. Five metropolitan areas have populations approaching or exceeding one million. Four are situated in the southeastern part of the country. The fifth is Perth, a coastal city in the southwestern corner of Australia.

With more than 3.4 million residents, Sydney is home to nearly 22 percent of the country's population. Established in 1788

as a colony for British prisoners, the settlement developed into a major seaport after farming products began to be exported. The long port, which has many bays, reaches inland for 21 miles, dividing the city into northern and southern sections. The Sydney Harbour Bridge, which opened in 1932, connects the two halves. Sydney is also Australia's largest manufacturing center.

Melbourne is the nation's second largest city, with about three million people. It is the capital of Victoria, the smallest mainland state. Founded in 1835, Melbourne grew rapidly after gold was discovered in Victoria in the 1850s. This business and industrial hub now offers many cultural opportunities. The city has three universities as well as fine museums and medical and scientific research institutions.

Brisbane, with a population of 1.2 million, sits in the southeastern corner of Queensland and is that state's capital. Great Britain founded Brisbane as a colony for convicts in 1823 and maintained it as a prison site until 1839. The British opened the town to free settlement in 1842. A warm climate helps the modern city attract tourists from southern Australia in winter.

Courtesy of Australian Information Service

Almost one quarter of Australia's population live in Sydney, whose most famous landmarks are the Opera House and the Harbour Bridge. The city's suburban area spreads almost 50 miles westward to the Blue Mountains.

Courtesy of Australian Information Service

Melbourne prides itself on its schools, theaters, galleries, and museums. The Victorian Arts Centre, marked by the modern spire of its theater building, reflects the city's interest in cultural activities.

Perth is the capital of Western Australia. With one million residents, the nation's fourth largest city lies on the Indian Ocean near the southwestern corner of the continent. Fifteen hundred miles of outback separate Perth from Adelaide, the closest large city. Perth has grown rapidly in recent years because of an increase in commercial activity and tourism. Western Australia's reserves of iron ore, oil, natural gas, bauxite, and other minerals are boosting Perth's economy and population.

Adelaide, the capital of South Australia, ranks fifth in population. Sheltered by the Mount Lofty Ranges, this city of 990,000 people has been an agricultural processing center for much of its history. By the 1980s, however, nonagricultural manufacturing was a greater source of jobs. Tourism is also important to the city's economy. Nearby Port Adelaide is a center for submarine manufacture.

Secondary Cities

The construction of Canberra, the capital of Australia, began in 1913. Situated in southeastern New South Wales, the city has 285,000 residents. In addition to governmental offices, Canberra contains many research institutes, the Australian National University, and a military college. The capital's land area forms the Australian Capital Territory (ACT), a political unit administered by the national government and separate from New South Wales. The nearby Territory of Jervis Bay is a strip of land set aside in 1915 that gives the ACT access to the sea.

Hobart, the capital of Tasmania, was founded in 1803 as a prison colony for lawbreakers who were repeat offenders. By the mid-1900s Hobart had become a major whaling port and boat-building site. With a population of 180,000, the city now serves as a center for both agriculture and industry. Tasmanian farms raise cattle, sheep, and apples and other fruit. Hobart's factories produce zinc, sulfuric acid, processed fruits, and paper.

Two important towns in the Northern Territory are Darwin, the region's capital, and Alice Springs. The former site is named for Charles Darwin, the famous British naturalist who landed there in 1839. With a population of 65,000, Darwin

Courtesy of Australian Information Service

Adelaide sits at the mouth of the Murray River. The city, which many people consider the most beautiful in Australia, is surrounded by hills. A broad greenbelt of parks, playing fields, and walking trails surround the center of Adelaide.

The High Court building in Canberra faces Lake Burley Griffin—named after Walter Burley Griffin, the U.S. architect who designed the city.

Courtesy of Australian Tourist Commission

sits at the northern edge of the outback. Mining in the Northern Territory has boosted Darwin's economic importance in recent years.

Alice Springs, at the southern end of the territory, is close to the geographical center of the continent. This town of about 25,000 residents is a center for the outback cattle industry. It is served by a rail line from Adelaide, by a north-south transcontinental highway, and by air routes. Also a tourist destination, Alice Springs is a departure point for trips to Ayers Rock, one of the the world's biggest rocks.

Hobart, the smallest of Australia's state capitals, lies on the southeastern coast of Tasmania beside the Derwent River. Hobart's climate is colder than that of other Australian urban areas.

Courtesy of Australian Information Service

19

A painting of a kangaroo is one of many Aboriginal artworks in Kakadu National Park, 150 miles east of Darwin. The wilderness park contains at least 300 Aboriginal art galleries, but as many as 1,000 more—known only to the Aborigines—may exist in the region. The earliest of the paintings that visitors can see are 18,000 years old. Many Aboriginal artworks were symbolic and could be fully understood only by the group that created them.

Photo by Kay Shaw Photography

2) History and Government

At least 40,000 years ago, Stone-Age peoples reached Australia from Southeast Asia. The migrations to Australia came in waves over hundreds of years. Centuries later, Europeans were to call these groups Aborigines. (The name comes from the Latin phrase *ab origine*, which means "from the beginning.")

The earliest migrants probably crossed a chain of islands that once linked Australia to the Asian mainland. Later groups might have traveled on rafts between islands now covered by water. Eventually, however, migrations ceased, and the Aborigines lived in isolation from other peoples for thousands of years.

Historians believe that ships from China, Arabia, and the islands of Indonesia sailed to Australia in the thirteenth century. Portuguese and Spanish navigators may have reached the continent in the sixteenth century. Not until the seventeenth century, however, did European explorers begin to map Australia's coast. Another century passed before a Western nation—Great Britain—claimed and settled the territory.

The First Australians

About 500 Aboriginal groups, each with a distinct language, established themselves in Australia. The Aborigines lived by hunting and gathering. Some families built shelters of branches and grasses, but they had no permanent dwellings. By the time Europeans began to colonize the continent in the late 1700s, the Aborigines numbered about 300,000. They lived primarily along the northern and eastern coasts and in the Murray River Valley. About 4,000 of them inhabited Tasmania.

Each Aboriginal group occupied a recognized territory. Within the boundaries of each territory, clans of 10 to 50 people roamed in search of food. The Aborigines obeyed strict family rules and customs, with the young and strong providing for the old and feeble. Men of high standing in each group led ceremonies and made decisions affecting their people.

Among the Aborigines' few possessions were digging sticks, bags for carrying food, and *didjeridoos*—musical instruments that produce a wailing sound. Their hunting weapons included boomerangs, traps, nets, barbed wooden spears, stone axes, and pointed sticks.

Following strict rituals that inflicted little harm, Aborigines used warfare to show their skill and daring. Meeting at traditional battle sites, warring groups would exchange insults and challenges and then hurl spears at the opposing side. By confronting the enemy and dodging weapons, each side achieved prestige.

According to the beliefs of the Aborigines, their ancestors created the world long ago in the Dreamtime. During religious ceremonies, men endured painful physical rituals that put them in a trance. While in this state, the Aborigines believed they entered the Dreamtime and could exchange thoughts with their ancestors—who at death had merged with nature. Through rock paintings and spoken legends, the people passed Dreamtime stories from one generation to the next.

Throughout history, male elders have provided leadership for Aboriginal bands, although the groups do not have official rulers.

Courtesy of Australian Tourist Commission

The Aborigines believed Ayers Rock, in Australia's Red Centre, was the place where everything began. Etched with deep gullies, the rock rises 1,260 feet from the desert plain. The distance around its base is six miles. Ayers Rock appears to change color with the time of day and weather.

Courtesy of Ruth Karl

European Discovery

Until the 1600s, foreign influences had little impact on Aboriginal culture. In the seventeenth century, however, expanding trade in Asia led European powers—particularly the Netherlands—to take a greater interest in the South Pacific. Many navigators believed in the legend of a "great south land," which they hoped would contain precious metals and spices.

In pursuit of this legendary continent, the Dutch navigator Willem Jansz reached northeastern Australia in 1606. Jansz thought the area was an unknown part of New Guinea, a large island north of Australia. Although his reports about the region and its people were discouraging, Dutch explorers continued to search for the great south land. In doing so, they charted much of the western coast of Australia. In 1642 Abel Tasman sailed around the continent and discovered Tasmania, which he named Van Diemen's Land, after a Dutch official. Tasman shared Jansz's unfavorable impressions of the area.

The Dutch explorations encouraged visits by other European navigators. The first British explorer to arrive in Australia was William Dampier, who journeyed there in 1688 and again in 1699. He, too, found the territory unpromising and doubted that it could be the great south land of legend. Interest in the continent lagged until 1770. In that year, Captain James Cook, exploring for the British navy, reached the southeastern corner of Australia. Cook charted the eastern coast.

On April 19, 1770, Cook's ship, the *Endeavour*, reached Botany Bay, which Cook named for the many unusual plants growing there. The navigator claimed the eastern part of the continent for Britain.

Courtesy of James Ford Bell Library, University of Minnesota

Captain James Cook claimed the eastern part of Australia for Britain in 1770. Cook sailed along the eastern coast as far north as Cape York. His account of the continent stirred considerable interest in Britain, but 18 years passed before the first British settlers—most of whom were prisoners—arrived in Australia.

Independent Picture Service

The Founding of Australia, painted by Algernon Talmage, shows the unfurling of the British flag at Sydney Cove on January 26, 1788, now celebrated as Australia Day. The artist depicts Captain Arthur Phillip, his officers, and his guard of marines about to drink the health of Britain's King George III. Their ship *Supply* is anchored in the cove.

Exploring the South Pacific again from 1772 to 1775, Cook proved that no landmass other than Australia could possibly be the great south land. The name Australia, from the Latin word for south, was first used by another British navigator, Matthew Flinders, who also surveyed the continent's coasts.

British Settlement

At first, the British made no attempt to colonize Australia. In 1783, however, the United States won its independence, and Britain lost 13 of its North American colonies. Until this time, Britain had used 2 of those colonies—Georgia and Maryland— as prisons for its convicts. Britain, which had few prisons, needed a new place to send people convicted of crimes. Officials decided the remote continent of Australia would suit the purpose.

After an eight-month journey from Britain, the first fleet of 11 ships arrived in Botany Bay in January 1788. The vessels carried 548 male and 188 female convicts and about 300 free persons, most of whom were soldiers serving as guards. Captain Arthur Phillip, the colony's governor, decided to move the fleet seven miles north to what he hoped would be a better harbor and richer soil. On January 26, 1788, the settlers arrived at what would become Sydney, New South Wales, and founded the first white settlement on the continent.

From the beginning, the colony at Sydney faced great difficulties. Phillip had expected that prisoners would soon be growing food. But the soil in the immediate area was poor. Wheat seeds had been damaged on the journey and failed to grow. Animals brought on the first fleet died or escaped. Convicts and their keepers alike were near starvation when a second fleet

Courtesy of Australian Tourist Commission

The prison ruins at Port Arthur stand as a reminder of Tasmania's beginnings as a prison colony. Convicts held there were repeat offenders, and a government report of 1837 said they endured beatings and wretched conditions. Punishment eventually became more humane, however, and some convicts spent their time at Port Arthur learning a trade. The prison was abandoned in 1877.

finally arrived 30 months after the first. The second fleet, however, had little food to spare, and many of its passengers were ill or dying.

To encourage farming, the governor began giving land to soldiers and to those convicts who had finished serving their terms. To obtain enough land, the officials seized territory from local Aborigines, offering no payments or treaties in return. A special military force called the New South Wales Corps came from Britain to serve in Australia. Officers and soldiers in the corps treated the convicts cruelly. Conditions were especially harsh on Norfolk Island, an outpost situated 1,000 miles

Photo by Emily Slowinski

Convicts built the Richmond Bridge on Tasmania in the 1820s. Local legend says the bridge is haunted by the spirit of a cruel overseer whom the convicts killed.

east of Australia that had been set up to hold second offenders and political prisoners. Some inmates there committed murder so that they would be hanged and escape their misery.

Early Reforms

In 1792 Captain Phillip returned to Britain, and officers of the New South Wales Corps gained power in the colony. The officers used their authority to enrich themselves. They acquired land and gained control of the rum trade. Rum, which was much in demand in the colony, came to serve as money. The officers of the New South Wales Corps came to be known as the Rum Corps. While the Rum Corps controlled affairs, little consideration was given to the rights and needs of freed convicts.

Reforms in Australia took hold, however, after Lachlan Macquarie became governor in 1810. Macquarie broke the monopoly of the Rum Corps and established a money system and a bank. He constructed public buildings and roads. Macquarie supported the rights of former convicts, many of whom became productive citizens after serving their prison terms and gaining their freedom.

In 1813 Macquarie also encouraged the first crossing of the Blue Mountains. Those mountains, which are a rugged chain in the Great Dividing Range, had confined settlement to a semicircle of land around Sydney. With a route open through the Blue Mountains, free settlers and colonial officers began occupying grasslands farther west.

Although the government claimed ownership of the land, the people moving in asserted their right to it by "squatting"—staking claim by living on the property. Some squatters seized huge tracts—as much as 20,000 acres. Frequently, they obtained land by killing the Aborigines who lived in the area or by using guns to drive them away.

Such actions by squatters added to the problems of the Aboriginal population,

Independent Picture Service

A view of Sydney a few years after its founding shows a number of structures built with convict labor. Francis Greenway, who had been sent to New South Wales for making false documents, became the colony's leading architect shortly after his arrival in 1814.

Independent Picture Service

In the early 1800s, European settlers began taking over lands that for thousands of years had been the recognized territories of Aboriginal groups. Some Aborigines fiercely resisted the more powerful newcomers, but eventually they were killed or forced to move onto lands of other Aboriginal peoples.

which began to shrink soon after Europeans settled in Australia. Many Aborigines died from smallpox and other diseases unknown to them before the British arrived. Liquor—which was easy to obtain in the colony—ruined the lives of many other Aborigines. The newcomers competed with the Aborigines for the dwindling supply of fish, and they drove away kangaroos and other game that the Aborigines hunted for food.

While the Aboriginal population disappeared from southeastern Australia, the region's squatters prospered. Most landholders began raising Merino sheep, a breed that could survive on dry vegetation. These sheep produced a fine wool that settlers could sell abroad.

Exploration and Expansion

As the settlement grew, explorers journeyed north of Sydney, discovering the Darling Downs area of southern Queensland and the Brisbane River. Two adventurers walked overland to the southern coast, arriving at what would become Melbourne. To prevent other European countries from settling Australia, Britain claimed the western half of the continent in 1829.

Independent Picture Service

In the early 1800s, livestock farmers found that Merino sheep, a breed that originally came from Spain, could thrive in Australia and that Merino wool could be a valuable export. The sheep are still very important to the country's economy.

26

Independent Picture Service

A bronze statue of Australian explorer Charles Sturt stands in Queen Victoria Square, Adelaide. Sturt explored the Murray River and its tributaries.

Setting out the same year, Captain Charles Sturt traced the course of the westward-flowing rivers and learned that Australia had no great inland sea, as some had thought it did. His was the first of many expeditions that would attempt to unlock the secrets of the continent's interior. Some explorers who challenged the outback became folk heroes. Others perished in their efforts to cross the hot, parched land.

The dry climate of inland Australia limited most settlement to the eastern border and southeastern corner of the continent and to edges of the western and northern coasts. Britain granted colonial status to Van Diemen's Land (now called Tasmania) in 1824. In the same year, Britain established a prison colony on the Brisbane River in Queensland, which remained a part of New South Wales. A settlement that sprang up in 1829 on the Swan River in Western Australia eventually became the city of Perth.

Sheep farmers from Tasmania founded Melbourne on the mainland in 1835. These squatters did well, and Britain later granted their request to form Victoria, a colony separate from New South Wales. The South Australia Company in London established the colony of South Australia, with its capital at Adelaide, in 1836. In

Independent Picture Service

Established in 1835, Melbourne was a thriving town by 1850. City planners set aside large areas for public parks. This view shows the Princess Bridge from the south side of the Yarra River.

addition to the British, South Australia's earliest settlers included Germans who were seeking freedom from religious persecution in their homeland.

The Gold Rush

Sheep raising and the export of wool to Britain dominated Australia's economy in the first half of the nineteenth century. In 1850 Australia had 18 million sheep and only 400,000 people. In 1851, however, Edward Hargreaves—a mining prospector returning from the California gold rush—discovered gold at Bathurst in New South Wales. By the end of the year, prospectors found bigger deposits in Victoria.

Until the gold discoveries, Australia had difficulty attracting enough immigrants to meet its labor needs. But the possibility of finding gold suddenly made people willing to travel the great distance to the South Pacific. Prospectors from Europe, the United States, and China came to the gold fields.

Administering the distant colonies in Australia was difficult and expensive for Great Britain. In 1855 the British Parliament passed legislation allowing the colonies to become largely self-governing while still under British authority. As a result, by 1859 the four eastern colonies— New South Wales, Victoria, South Australia, and Tasmania—had adopted constitutions and had formed their own governments. Queensland separated from New South Wales in 1859 and also became responsible for its own government. (Western Australia did not adopt limited self-government until 1890.)

The gold rush had helped to promote a sense of social equality among Australians.

Courtesy of Australian Tourist Commission

German immigrants settled South Australia's Barossa Valley, bringing wine-making expertise from Europe. The valley is now one of the top wine-producing districts of Australia.

Courtesy of Australian Information Service

The discovery of gold *(above)* in the early 1850s drew a flood of immigrants who helped double Australia's population to one million within 10 years. The gold fields attracted people of all social classes *(below)* and broke down social barriers.

Independent Picture Service

Gulgong, a typical gold-rush town in the 1870s, boasted a newspaper office, a hairdresser's shop, a tobacconist's store, and well-dressed citizens.

Independent Picture Service

Becoming wealthy by striking gold did not depend on one's family background. In fact, persons who were accustomed to hard physical work had an advantage over fortune hunters who were not used to manual labor. In addition, living conditions in the gold fields were rugged for everyone and blurred class barriers. Throughout Australia, members of the working class began to fill seats in the colonial parliaments.

By drawing people of widely different occupations to Australia, the discovery of gold paved the way for industrialization. The gold rush also helped boost the population past one million by 1860. With a more abundant labor supply, large landholders no longer needed British convicts. Changing conditions in Britain had also lessened the need for overseas prisons. As a result, the shipping of convicts to

Independent Picture Service

Women, who were greatly outnumbered by men in Australia, shared the hardships of pioneering in the late 1800s. Many maintained their households in earthen dwellings with thatched roofs. New immigrants lacked family networks and relied on neighbors for social contact.

Independent Picture Service

A painting by Tom Roberts depicts the opening of the first Australian Parliament in May 1901 by Britain's Duke of Cornwall and York—later King George V. His wife (later Queen Mary) stands behind him.

Australia—a practice that had brought 160,000 people to the colony—ended in 1868.

Forming One Nation

Soon after achieving limited self-rule, the colonies began holding regular conferences that gave the prime ministers a chance to discuss common concerns, such as taxing imports. Considerable rivalries existed among the colonies, however, and close cooperation and political union did not develop until economic disaster threatened Australia in the 1890s.

Early in that decade, the colonies experienced an economic depression. As people lost their jobs, membership in trade unions increased. The unions formed political parties in each colony to push for laws that would help working people. These labor parties wanted the colonies to unite because they believed that standardized labor laws would benefit workers.

Spurred also by their need for common immigration laws and tariff (import-tax)

policies, the colonies decided to form a federation. This system of government gives most powers to the national government but reserves some authority for the states. In 1897 delegates to a national convention began to draw up a constitution, which voters in all the colonies accepted by 1899. Britain approved the plan in 1900, and the Commonwealth of Australia was formally established on January 1, 1901. Melbourne served as the capital temporarily while the government built the permanent capital of Canberra, which was finished in 1927.

Although the new federation was an independent nation, rivalries among the former colonies continued after they became the six states of Australia. In some ways the states trusted Britain more than they trusted one another. For this reason, even after independence they chose to maintain political ties to Britain. Australia was a member of the British Commonwealth and recognized Britain's monarch as its own. Britain still exercised authority over Australia's foreign policy, and British laws could overrule legislation that had been enacted by the Australian Parliament.

In 1901 the new government adopted immigration laws that virtually excluded non-European immigrants from Australia for more than 50 years. Unofficially known as the White Australia policy, the legislation reflected a strain of racial prejudice among Australians that first surfaced during the gold rush.

When Australia was established, about 60,000 Aborigines survived in the country. The new federal and state governments adopted policies to protect Aborigines but did not give them rights of citizenship. Most of them lived on reserves in the barren Northern Territory and in Queensland, away from white Australians. In general, the government ignored the needs of these people, who came to depend on churches and other private groups for assistance.

Courtesy of Australian Tourist Commission

In the first decades after Australia gained independence, most Aborigines lived in rural areas, and many white Australians believed the ethnic group had become extinct. On Tasmania, in fact, all Aborigines did die out.

The World Wars

Australia's political ties to Britain had an important effect in 1914. In that year, Britain declared war against Germany, which meant that Australia was at war as well. The country sent more than 330,000 soldiers to Europe and northern Africa to fight in World War I (1914–1918). Australians and New Zealanders fought jointly as the Anzac forces (Australian and New Zealand Army Corps). For these troops, the most famous battle of the war began when they landed in Gallipoli, Turkey, on April 25, 1915. The war was costly for Australia in human terms. Nearly 60,000 Australians lost their lives. Yet, their achievements in the war helped Australians develop a sense of common purpose and of nationhood.

World War I strengthened Australia economically as well as politically. The demand for wartime goods encouraged manufacturing and boosted exports of food, minerals, and wool. European immigration to Australia resumed after the war, and the 1920s brought improvements in the standard of living. The nation built more roads to accommodate a growing number of cars. The cities acquired electric trains. Telegraph lines, telephones, and airmail letter service put Australians in closer touch with other areas of the world.

A global depression in the 1930s, however, created trouble for Australia's economy. In some cities, 30 percent of the people lost their jobs, and immigration virtually ceased. So sparsely settled was their continent that many Australians feared the country had too few people to survive.

When World War II broke out in 1939, Australians again aided Britain in its fight against Germany. Britain and its allies were soon at war not only in Europe but in the Pacific against Japan. The threat that Japan would invade Australia was very real. After the British colony of Singapore fell to the Japanese in February 1942, Australians realized that British forces in the Pacific could not protect them

Australian and New Zealand soldiers fought together as the Anzac forces during World War I (1914–1918). In December 1915 the troops were engaged in heroic, but finally unsuccessful, fighting to take the Gallipoli Peninsula in western Turkey. Nearly 60,000 Australians lost their lives in the war.

Photo by Imperial War Museum

from invasion. Australia turned to the United States for help.

John Curtin, the Australian prime minister, placed Australia's forces under the command of a U.S. general. One million U.S. soldiers moved into the country, whose own population was only seven million. Japanese planes bombed Darwin and Broome, Australia, in early 1942, and Japan seemed to be winning the war in the Pacific. But in May 1942, a combined U.S.-Australian fleet won an important victory in the Battle of the Coral Sea, and the tide began to turn against Japan. Fighting continued for three more years before Japan agreed on August 14, 1945 to end the war.

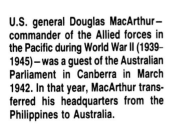

U.S. general Douglas MacArthur—commander of the Allied forces in the Pacific during World War II (1939–1945)—was a guest of the Australian Parliament in Canberra in March 1942. In that year, MacArthur transferred his headquarters from the Philippines to Australia.

Courtesy of MacArthur Memorial

Courtesy of Australian Information Service

The width of the continent separates Perth, the capital of Western Australia, from other major cities. After World War II, the city prospered as the center for the state's mining ventures. During a high-rise building boom in the 1970s and 1980s, Perth managed to preserve historic examples of colonial architecture. Perth is the third busiest port in Australia.

Postwar Growth and Prosperity

After the war, Australia and the United States strengthened the close relationship they had developed during their wartime cooperation. With New Zealand as a third partner, they signed the ANZUS (Australia, New Zealand, United States) pact for mutual defense. To further protect its interests, Australia also became a founding member of the United Nations in 1949.

A long period of political stability began in 1949 when Robert Menzies became prime minister. Menzies was leader of the Liberal party, which had formed during World War II to oppose some of the Labour party's policies. Menzies took an active interest in Pacific and Southeast Asian affairs. Under his leadership, the White Australia immigration policy began to change, and by 1973 it was abandoned.

Labor shortages existed after the war, and most Australians believed that for safety and continued prosperity, their country needed more people. To encourage immigration, the government offered incentives—such as free land and assistance with transportation expenses—to people in other countries. As a result, two million immigrants arrived in the 1950s and 1960s. Southern Europeans made up the bulk of the newcomers in the 1950s. The influx of these new ethnic groups began to diversify Australian society. In recent years, the country has welcomed thousands of refugees and others from Southeast Asia, Lebanon, Central and South America, and Africa.

In the 1960s, the Aborigines finally gained full citizenship, including the right to vote. Australians elected to give the national government, rather than the states, responsibility for Aboriginal affairs. The government began to involve Aborigines in decisions affecting their land, housing, health, education, and employment.

The 1970s

From 1949 to 1972, the Liberal and National parties—the more conservative of Australia's political organizations—controlled Parliament. The 1950s and the 1960s were generally decades of prosperity for the country. The economic boom was fueled in part by the development of mining in Western Australia.

In the early 1970s, however, world demand for the output of Australia's mines dropped, hurting the country's economy.

Labor strikes also added to the nation's financial problems. In some cases, workers won pay hikes that were not matched by increases in productivity (output). As labor costs increased, manufacturers had to raise prices on Australian-made goods.

In addition, political and social issues disrupted Australia in the 1970s. Groups demonstrated against the country's involvement in the Vietnam war and against the government's support for U.S. policies in Southeast Asia. Members of the women's movement sought greater participation for women in Australian political and business life. Other activists attempted to raise public concern about the social problems and land rights of the Aborigines.

In 1972, amid social protests and economic problems, national elections brought

Courtesy of Australian Information Service

In a ceremony at Wattie Creek, Northern Territory, in August 1975, Prime Minister Gough Whitlam presented a handful of soil to Vincent Lingiari, leader of the Gurindji Aborigines. The gesture symbolized the return of ownership of 1,250 square miles of grazing land. The occasion, which ended a nine-year land-rights struggle, was the first transfer of territory back to Aborigines since Europeans came to Australia.

Independent Picture Service

Malcolm Fraser, head of the Liberal party, was prime minister of Australia from 1975 to 1983.

believed Whitlam's programs were too expensive. Eventually, Parliament refused to pass bills that required government funding.

Because Parliament and the prime minister could not agree on a course of action, the governor-general, Sir John Kerr, took a step that many Australians believed was illegal. Using his formal authority as the representative of the British monarch, he dismissed Whitlam in November 1975. Kerr then installed Malcolm Fraser, the head of the Liberal party, as prime minister. General elections were held the following month. Voters showed their approval of Fraser by giving the two parties backing him – the Liberal and the National parties – the largest margin of victory in Australian history. Fraser was reelected in December 1977.

the Labour party to power. Led by Gough Whitlam, the Labour government started many progressive social programs. However, the prime minister enacted these changes at a time when the country could not afford to pay for them. Unemployment was high, and foreign trade earnings were dropping. Many members of Parliament

The Hawke Era

The Labour party regained power in 1983— another time of economic difficulty—and Robert Hawke became prime minister. In an effort to improve the economy, Hawke held a meeting of business, union, and government leaders in Canberra. The three

Courtesy of Australian Tourist Commission

The Australian coat of arms on the High Court building in Canberra overlooks modern structures along University Avenue. The six state crests are represented on the coat of arms and are supported by two native animals, the kangaroo and the emu.

Photo by UPI/Bettmann Newsphotos

President George Bush of the United States welcomed Prime Minister Robert Hawke of Australia on the south lawn of the White House in June 1989. In foreign policy, Hawke has been a strong supporter of U.S. actions.

groups signed an accord to cooperate for the good of the whole society. The accord reduced the frequency of labor strikes and spurred economic growth.

During Whitlam's reforms in the early 1970s, Aboriginal land rights became a political cause backed by many Australians. In the Northern Territory, Aborigines claim or have been granted 48 percent of the land. In 1985 a well-known area containing Ayers Rock was returned to the Aborigines. Since that time, however, the movement to return land to the Aborigines has slowed. Mining companies have developed much of the disputed territory. These firms claim that their use of the land entitles them to retain ownership.

The land-rights issue has also been overshadowed by the country's economic problems. The Australian standard of living fell during the 1980s. The country coped with unemployment and inflation. But Australians showed their confidence in the Hawke government by reelecting the Labour party in 1984 and again in 1987. Hawke continued to have generally good relations with both the business sector and with trade unions. In August 1989, however, domestic airline pilots went on strike. As the work stoppage continued into 1990, Australia's tourism industry lost a large amount of business. The situation indicated that the country's long tradition of labor problems had not ended.

37

Government

Australia has governments at the federal, state, and local levels. Parliament handles matters of national interest as set forth in a written constitution. That document also specifies which powers the national government shares with the states. All other authority is reserved for the states. The British monarch, who is also the monarch of Australia, is represented by the Australian governor-general and by six state governors, all of whom perform largely symbolic functions.

Each of Australia's six states administers its own system of education, transportation, law enforcement, health services, and agriculture. The federal government collects all taxes and gives a share to each state. States needing additional funds to provide services must apply to the national government.

The federal Parliament consists of the House of Representatives and the Senate. The House has 148 members. In the Senate, which is modeled after that of the United States, each state has 12 senators, and the Australian Capital Territory and the Northern Territory each have two.

Senators serve six-year terms. Except on bills relating to financial matters, the Senate has the same authority as the House in legislation.

Voters, who must be at least 18 years old, normally choose national representatives every three years. The party or coalition (combination) of parties with a majority in the House of Representatives runs the government and chooses the ministry—prime minister and cabinet—from its membership. The ministry can continue in office as long as Parliament continues to pass bills that the ministry proposes.

The High Court of Australia—consisting of a chief justice and six other justices—is at the top of the judicial system. It hears appeals from lower courts and cases involving the interpretation of the constitution. Australia has both state and federal court systems. Magistrates' courts in each state handle minor offenses without a jury. District or county courts hear criminal and some civil cases. The supreme courts of each state and of the Northern Territory deal with the most important civil and criminal offenses. They also serve as courts of appeal for cases from lower courts.

The Australian flag portrays the British flag in the upper lefthand corner. On the blue field beneath it is the seven-pointed Commonwealth star representing the six states and the Northern Territory. The right half of the flag contains the five stars of the Southern Cross, a constellation in the Southern Hemisphere.

Artwork by Laura Westlund

Photo by Sandi and Jim Provencher

Five-year-olds at a private school in suburban Sydney listen to their teacher's instructions while lining up to run a relay race. Most Australian children begin school before the compulsory age of six by attending preschool and transition (kindergarten) classes.

3) The People

From 1950 to 1990 Australia's population more than doubled, increasing from about 7 million to 16.8 million. Forty percent of the growth resulted from immigration, which the government actively encouraged from 1945 to 1965. About one in five Australians was born overseas.

The country's population density—five people per square mile—is one of the lowest in the world. Yet, Australia is one of the most urbanized countries, since 85 percent of its people live in cities and towns. Three-quarters of the urban residents are concentrated in the eight cities that serve as capitals for the six states, the nation, and the Northern Territory. The desert and semidesert regions that make up two-

thirds of Australia's land area are very sparsely populated.

Ethnic Mixture

From the early 1800s until the late 1940s, all but a small number of white Australians were of British descent. Most who were not could trace their ancestry to other countries of northern Europe. The Aborigines, whose population dropped to less than 25,000 by 1860, lived mainly in remote areas of the continent apart from white Australians.

Faced with labor shortages after World War II ended in 1945, Australia attempted to increase its population by paying travel

39

expenses or by giving land to people willing to settle there. Half the immigrants who took advantage of the offer were British, but newcomers also arrived from Poland, the Netherlands, West Germany, Yugoslavia, Italy, Greece, and other countries. The new immigration policy brought ethnic and cultural diversity to Australia.

Until recent years, few Asians made their homes in Australia. Although the gold rush of the 1850s had attracted about 40,000 Chinese to the country, few established permanent residence. From the 1880s to the early 1970s, Australia's immigration laws discriminated against Asians who wanted to move to Australia. By 1973 these laws had been abolished.

Since then, Australia has accepted many Asian refugees, including large numbers from Vietnam, Laos, and Cambodia. Other refugees have come from Eastern Europe, Latin America, the Middle East, and Africa. One-fourth of the immigrants who were admitted during the 1980s were

Photo by Kay Shaw Photography

A guide cooks lunch for tourists in Litchfield Park, a nature reserve southwest of Darwin. Outdoor barbecues—called barbies—are a favorite pastime in Australia.

Asians, and people of Asian backgrounds now make up about 4 percent of Australia's population.

Since 1982 job shortages and economic problems have caused the country to severely restrict immigration. The govern-

Independent Picture Service

An Aboriginal cattleman reins in his horse at Yandeyarra Station, a ranch near Port Hedland, Western Australia. The cattle industry of the outback has been a major source of employment for rural Aborigines.

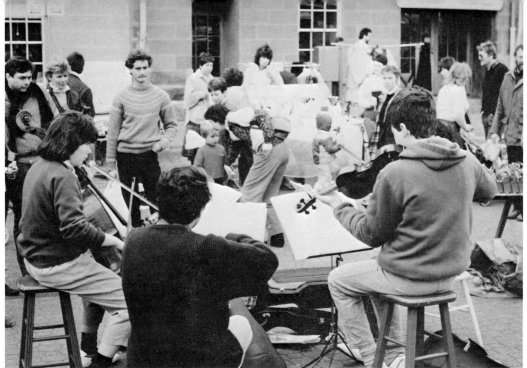

Photo by Emily Slowinski

Street musicians play at the Salamanca Place market in Hobart, Tasmania. Dating from the 1830s, this area of warehouses has been restored and is now occupied by restaurants, art studios, crafts workshops, and boutiques.

ment now grants permanent residence to only four categories of people—close relatives of Australian citizens, investors in new industries, skilled or specially qualified individuals, and selected refugees.

Standard of Living

White, working Australians are accustomed to a high standard of living. About 72 percent of the nation's families buy their own homes, and most families have at least one car. Australians travel frequently, and many who live in the outback fly their own light aircraft. Most Australians work 35 to 38 hours per week and each year receive at least four weeks' vacation and 10 paid holidays. Workers receive 17.5 percent extra pay while they are on vacation.

Australians spend much of their leisure time out of doors. They favor an informal lifestyle, and outdoor barbecues are a favorite form of recreation. Social status is related to earning power, rather than to family background. Decades of labor short-

ages enabled unskilled workers to command good wages. As a result, incomes tend to be high overall.

For many years, Australian women worked as housewives and mothers and were underrepresented in professions and in public life. Men often spent little time

Courtesy of Australian Information Service

Since the late 1970s, women have worked alongside men in the iron-ore mines of Western Australia.

About 72 percent of Australia's householders own their own homes. Individual brick houses with tiled roofs, such as these dwellings, are very popular in suburban Canberra. Industry and exports are the basis of Australia's high standard of living.

Courtesy of Australian Information Service

with their families and regarded their primary role as that of wage earner. More women began to enter the work force in the 1960s, and in 1973 a law granted federal employees the right to maternity leave. By 1985 women comprised 40 percent of the work force.

Most of Australia's Aborigines have a much lower standard of living than the rest of the population. About two-thirds of the country's 160,000 Aborigines now make their homes in urban areas. Those in rural communities live mainly in the Northern Territory, Western Australia, and Queensland. Many rural Aborigines still follow the religion, laws, and social organization that their culture developed thousands of years ago.

Most urban Aborigines do not have adequate housing or income, and poverty leads to major health problems. Since the early 1970s, the government has stepped up its programs to provide medical care, legal aid, and economic assistance to Aboriginal groups. With government backing, Aborigines developed and operate a large cattle station (ranch) in Queensland. Other programs have helped Aborigines set up their own small businesses.

In recent years, Aborigines have begun to express pride in their traditional culture more openly. New forms of Aboriginal arts are emerging in written and oral literature, dance, art, music, film, poetry, and drama. Many Aborigines find an outlet for creative expression at *corroborees,* social gatherings that are highlighted by music and dancing.

Education and Religion

School attendance is compulsory for Australian children between the ages of six and fifteen (sixteen in Tasmania). Most children, however, begin attending preschool at age four or five. Two-thirds of Australia's youth attend public schools, and the remainder enroll in private schools sponsored by Protestant or Roman Catholic churches.

A few private Protestant schools that are patterned after British private schools have gained reputations as elite institutions. Many Australian leaders in government, business, and professional careers have graduated from these schools.

Secondary schooling begins after six or seven years of primary education and can

42

continue for six more years. Many Australian students, however, leave school after four years of secondary education. Only 40 percent of Australia's 17-year-olds attend school, compared to 80 percent in the United States. Students who complete the final two years of secondary studies can qualify for entry to the country's 19 universities or to about 50 colleges and institutes for advanced education. Australia has a 98 percent literacy rate.

Most Aboriginal children attend the same schools as other Australian children. In recognition of the Aborigines' unique cultural heritage, however, the government offers them special preschool programs, advisers, and courses. In areas with a high percentage of Aborigines,

Aboriginal and white children share a classroom at an elementary school in Batchelor, between Hodgson Downs and Darwin.

Photo by Chris Fairclough

Courtesy of Australian Information Service

Pupils receive instruction on a computer at a public elementary school in Sydney.

courses are taught in both the Aboriginal language and English.

Although many Australians do not attend church regularly, most are Christians. Of these, 26 percent belong to the Anglican Church and 26 percent are Roman Catholic. Among non-Christian religions, the Islamic, Jewish, and Buddhist faiths have the largest followings in Australia.

Medical and Social Services

Private doctors and medical personnel provide most health care in Australia, but Medicare, the nation's health insurance program, covers most medical expenses. The government funds Medicare through income tax collections. Treatment in public hospitals is free, and private insurance programs cover charges in private facilities. Australia's life expectancy of 76 years reflects the nation's high standard of health care.

Since 1927 the Flying Doctor Service has provided medical aid to persons in sparsely populated regions of the continent. Two-way radios link two-thirds of the country to bases that can dispatch medical aircraft.

The government provides a variety of social services. The elderly, the long-term ill or handicapped, and single parents receive pensions (regular income payments). Cash payments are also made to the unemployed, the sick, and those with special needs. All families with children receive an allowance for each child under 16 and for each full-time student under 25, regardless of the family's earnings. Low-income families also receive financial assistance.

Courtesy of Australian Information Service

A physician and helpers load an injured workman aboard an aircraft of the Broken Hill Flying Doctor Service in western New South Wales. In addition to handling emergencies in the outback, flying doctors make calls at small hospitals and give medical treatment and advice at field clinics. The Broken Hill base serves an area of 215,000 square miles.

44

Traditionally, Australians have looked to their government to provide assistance in periods of economic need. At times during the 1970s and 1980s, the level of unemployment was high, and many Australians were "on the dole"—as dependence on government payments is called. In the late 1980s, unemployment declined, however, as businesses began to generate new jobs.

Literature

Australia's natural environment and history have inspired a large literary output. Nineteenth-century authors chronicled the country's prison-colony beginnings and natural habitats. Writing in the mid-1800s, Marcus Clarke depicted prison life in his best-known novel, *For the Term of His Natural Life.* In 1888 Thomas Alexander Browne described a gang of outlaws in *Robbery Under Arms.* The farmer Joseph Furphy used the diary form to express Australian attitudes in *Such is the Life,* which was published in 1903. In the 1920s, Ethel Richardson, writing under the name Henry Handel Richardson, gained fame abroad for her trilogy, *The Fortunes of Richard Mahoney,* about an Irish doctor who hated Australian life.

A major contemporary Australian writer is Patrick White, who won the 1973 Nobel Prize for literature. Among his widely read works is *Voss,* the story of a German who attempts to explore the interior of Australia. In recent years, the novels of Elizabeth Jolley have earned praise from literary critics in Europe and the United States.

Australia has produced many other highly regarded writers. Among the best known are Cristina Stead, Thomas Keneally, Morris West, Peter Carey, and Michael Wilding. Colleen McCullough's popular novel *The Thorn Birds* introduced millions of readers throughout the world to the Australian outback. Germaine Greer, who was born and educated in Australia, is well known for her writing on feminist issues.

Courtesy of The Nobel Foundation

Patrick White received a Nobel Prize for literature in 1973. Born in 1912, White is one of Australia's greatest novelists. His books include *Tree of Man* and *Signal Driver.*

Australia has been home to many notable poets. No poetry, however, has been more popular than the ballads of Andrew Barton Paterson. "Waltzing Matilda," which he wrote in 1917, is still the unofficial national song. Paterson's best-known ballads are contained in *The Man From Snowy River.* Modern Australian poets who have established their names in literary circles are Judith Wright, A. D. Hope, James McAuley, Douglas Stewart, and Kath Walker.

Sports and Recreation

Sports activities are an important part of Australian life. The country competes in

Courtesy of Australian Tourist Commission

Surfing is a favorite pastime for thousands of Australians, many of whom compete in surfing contests throughout the world.

the Olympic Games and has produced world champions in many fields of athletics. At least one-third of the Australian population register to participate in organized sports. In addition, many other Australians enjoy activities such as horseback riding, fishing, bushwalking (hiking), boating, cycling, and fitness programs.

The most popular winter spectator sport is Australian rules football—a uniquely Australian, fast-moving game with long kicks and leaping catches. The sport attracts 500,000 amateur participants each year. Almost as many Australians play soccer, which newly arrived European immigrants made popular after World War II.

In recent years, an Australian team (the Kangaroos) has dominated international competition in rugby, a game of British origin from which U.S. football is derived.

Britain is Australia's greatest rival in the sport, which is especially popular in New South Wales and Queensland. Sydney is the center for rugby league—a semiprofessional version that provides teams for international matches. Rugby union, which draws fewer spectators, is played by amateurs.

Cricket is the country's most played and watched summer sport. Thousands of fans attend matches that bring teams from other Commonwealth nations to Australia. Horse racing is the nation's oldest sport, since an official race was run near Sydney in 1810. The Melbourne Cup race, perhaps Australia's best-known sporting event, has been held since 1861.

Yachting is also an important activity in Australia, and Australians have designed some of the world's fastest yachts.

Courtesy of Australian Information Service

Australian rules football—a game similar to rugby but unique to Australia—is a popular winter spectator sport. Enthusiasm for the game is particularly strong in Melbourne, where 100,000 fans turn out for the season's championship.

Horses and riders move to the starting gate for the Melbourne Cup, Australia's premier horse race. The event is so popular that businesses and government offices suspend work for the running of the race, which carries $1 million in prize money.

Courtesy of Australian Information Service

Girls painted as clowns participate in a picnic and races at Noosa, a resort town on the "Sunshine Coast," which lies north of Brisbane.

Courtesy of Australian Tourist Commission

Cricket dominates Australian sports from October to March. Teams from every state but Tasmania play each other twice each season for the Sheffield Shield, Australia's top cricket prize. International matches are held in state capitals against England or another cricket-playing country every other year.

Courtesy of Australian Information Service

Courtesy of Australian Information Service

Evonne Goolagong Cawley, who is part Aborigine, was an important figure in international tennis competition in the 1970s. She won the Australian Women's Open tennis title in 1974.

One of the greatest moments in Australia's sports history occurred in September 1983 when the *Australia II* won the America's Cup, the greatest prize in yachting. The Australian yacht was the first foreign craft in 132 years to defeat the U.S. entry.

In individual competition, swimmers, runners, golfers, and tennis players have brought Australia fame. Fans of women's tennis recognize the feats of Evonne Goolagong Cawley and Margaret Smith Court. Between 1952 and 1974, Australian men won the Wimbledon singles tennis title 14 times. In the late 1980s, Greg Norman was one of the world's top professional golfers.

Art, Films, and Music

Australian painters in the late 1800s were strongly influenced by French painters of the same period. Frederick McCubbin and Tom Roberts used the impressionist style to depict Australian frontier life. Artists in the twentieth century include Sir Wil-

Courtesy of Atlantic Records

INXS is one of many Australian bands that were popular on the international rock-music scene during the 1980s.

48

liam Dobell, known for his portraits, and Sidney Nolan, who used themes from Australian folklore for his dreamlike paintings. George Russell Drysdale and Frederick Williams painted landscapes from the outback. In recent years, John Olsen and Brett Whiteley have gained international reputations. Albert Namatjira, an Aborigine, adopted European techniques and painted scenes of the Australian desert.

Australian filmmakers produce about 20 feature-length films each year, and most are distributed overseas. The country's famous stage and movie stars include Judith Anderson, Errol Flynn, Cyril Ritchard, Mel Gibson, and Paul Hogan. Australia has also made significant contributions to the international music scene. Australian-born musicians include sopranos Nellie Melba and Joan Sutherland, guitarist John Williams, and composer Percy Grainger. Popular rock artists include Olivia Newton-John, Rick Springfield, the Bee Gees, Air Supply, AC/DC, and INXS.

Independent Picture Service

An Aboriginal artist paints traditional symbols—including dots and geometric patterns—on the branch of a tree.

Courtesy of Richard Southward

The roofs of the Sydney Opera House, internationally famous for its innovative design, resemble billowing sails. Completed in 1973 at a cost of $100 million, the building contains a 1,700-seat main hall, a 1,550-seat auditorium, a small theater, and other rooms.

Courtesy of Australian Information Service

An offshore rig on the Northwest Shelf drills for natural gas. With supplies from its offshore wells and from inland gas fields, Australia meets most of its own requirements for this form of energy.

4) The Economy

Before World War II, Australia's economy depended largely on the production and export of agricultural goods. The war created a demand for many manufactured items, and Australian industries grew. Despite a labor shortage, factories continued to expand after the war ended in 1945.

To attract more workers in the postwar period, the government encouraged immigration. The strong demand for labor enabled both skilled and unskilled jobholders to earn high wages. In the 1960s, the discovery and development of mining and energy resources added to the country's prosperity.

Mostly as a result of changes in the world economy, however, Australia's economic growth faltered in the 1970s and early 1980s. Foreign demand for the country's minerals and metals fell, and the market for its agricultural products shrank. Unemployment rose, as did the cost of living.

From 1984 to 1988, Australia borrowed a great deal of money from outside sources, and the country accumulated a large foreign debt. Businesses and individuals who wanted to borrow money in Australia had to pay very high interest rates. Despite these facts, Australia's economy had improved by the end of the 1980s. Unemployment declined from 10 percent in 1983 to less than 6 percent in 1989.

In the past 20 years, most new jobs in Australia have opened in the service sector. This area of the economy includes retail and wholesale businesses, communications, financial institutions, entertainment and recreation industries, and government services. Services (including all levels of government) now employ two-thirds of the Australian work force. One out of four Australians holds a government job.

Mining and Manufacturing

Australia is rich in mineral, metal, and energy resources. The country is the world's leading exporter of coal and aluminum and a major producer of bauxite—the compound from which aluminum is made. Australia is also one of the top producers and exporters of iron ore, copper, nickel, gold, lead and zinc, diamonds, tin, tungsten, manganese, and zircon. Most high-quality opals come from a desert region in South Australia. Large reserves of uranium—a metal used to produce nuclear energy—exist in Australia.

Many of the country's richest mineral and ore deposits lie in remote, dry areas of the continent. Developing these resources was very expensive, since it required new roads, railways, and towns to house workers. To obtain money, mining companies turned to investors in other countries. As a result, foreigners own about half the stock in Australia's mining companies.

In 1961 geologists discovered oil 180 miles west of Brisbane, and commercial production began in 1964. Drillers found additional deposits of oil and natural gas

Courtesy of Australian Tourist Commission

In the northern part of Western Australia, giant shovels and ore trucks literally move mountains to extract minerals. The discovery of extensive mineral deposits has created major economic activity in this remote area of the state.

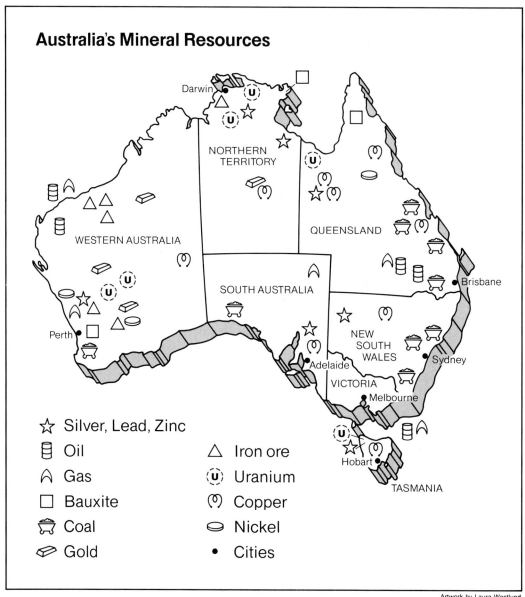

Australia's Mineral Resources

NORTHERN TERRITORY

Darwin

WESTERN AUSTRALIA

QUEENSLAND

SOUTH AUSTRALIA

Brisbane

Perth

NEW SOUTH WALES

Adelaide

Sydney

VICTORIA

Melbourne

Hobart

TASMANIA

☆ Silver, Lead, Zinc

🛢 Oil

⋀ Gas

▢ Bauxite

⛏ Coal

◇ Gold

△ Iron ore

Ⓤ Uranium

(ᑫ) Copper

⊖ Nickel

• Cities

Artwork by Laura Westlund

Australia's wealth of mineral resources has made the country a basic source of raw materials for export throughout the world. This map shows major mining centers of the country's most important minerals.

in Bass Strait, in the coastal waters of Western Australia, and in desert basins of both the Northern Territory and South Australia. The Bass Strait site contains immense reserves of petroleum.

Australia's factories make most of the consumer products the country needs. Nevertheless, the country must import most of the industrial machines and tools necessary to make these goods. Its leading manufactured products are processed foods, iron and other metals, transportation equipment, paper, chemicals, clothing, shoes, and household appliances. Sydney and Melbourne are the leading manufacturing centers.

An iron worker watches as molten metal fills an engine mold at an automotive factory in Melbourne.

Courtesy of Australian Information Service

For many years the Australian government protected the country's manufacturers from foreign competition by enacting high tariffs. Prime Minister Hawke changed that policy in the mid-1980s, and most tariffs were reduced. As a result, Australian manufacturers now face more competition from foreign companies in selling products to Australians.

Agriculture

Only 5 percent of Australians are farmers, but they grow almost all the food Australians need. They also produce wool, meat, grains, sugar, fruit, and dairy products for sale abroad. Although farms and large ranches cover 63 percent of Australia, 90 percent of the country's farmland is so dry that it can be used only as pasture. For this

Courtesy of General Motors-Holden Automotive Limited

The Holden is the most popular car in Australia. The Australian company that produces it is a part of General Motors, the U.S. car manufacturer. This model is the Holden Nova.

53

Photo by Emily Slowinski

Sheep graze on a hillside on the Tasman Peninsula. Since the first years of European settlement, the animals – which now number 150 million – have been vital to the Australian economy. No country has more sheep than Australia.

Courtesy of Australian Information Service

A cattleman corrals livestock in northern New South Wales. Australia is the world's largest exporter of beef and veal.

54

Courtesy of Australian Tourist Commission

Western Victoria produces rich harvests of wheat, a grain that Australia sells to many countries.

reason, pastoralism (livestock raising) dominates agriculture. The remaining 10 percent of the farmland produces crops. The most fertile soil lies in a 200-mile-wide crescent-shaped band in the country's southeastern corner.

Despite a gradual decline in Australia's rural population, scientific and technical advances have pushed farm output steadily upward. In some years, however, poor weather conditions have harmed agriculture. A drought in eastern Australia in 1982 and 1983 killed crops and many livestock and worsened economic conditions. Fires started by lightning can spread rapidly across dry scrublands, destroying whole farms in their paths. Prolonged lack of rain is not the only danger facing rural Australians. At times, flash floods threaten both people and animals.

55

Independent Picture Service

Shearing season demands long hours of hard work from sheep ranchers and their employees. Good shearers can clip more than 300 sheep per day.

Independent Picture Service

A grape picker seems pleased with the harvest in the Barossa Valley of South Australia, a state that produces 75 percent of Australia's wine grapes.

Sheep remain Australia's single most important agricultural product. Most of their value is in wool production, but some of the animals are raised for meat as well. The Merino breed, which produces a very fine grade of wool, makes up 70 percent of the country's sheep population. Ninety-seven percent of Australia's wool is exported, principally to Japan, the Soviet Union, and Europe.

Wheat, the country's largest grain crop, grows in all six states. Most of the wheat is shipped abroad to China, Egypt, the Soviet Union, and Japan. Australian farmers also cultivate other grains, such as barley, oats, sorghum, rye, and millet. Sugar is produced in Queensland and New South Wales. Growers harvest a variety of fruits in coastal orchards and vineyards. The big-

Courtesy of Australian Information Service

Fishermen at Port Lincoln transfer tuna from the hold to the deck of their boat. A machine will lift steel baskets full of fish to trucks on the wharf.

gest crops are grapes, citrus fruits, apples, bananas, pears, peaches, and pineapples.

Fishing and Forestry

Many species of fish live in Australia's coastal waters, but tuna and salmon for canning have the greatest commercial importance. For export, Australia's small fishing industry relies primarily on shellfish, including prawns, rock lobsters, abalone, and scallops. Japan and the United

Divers unload their day's catch of abalone. Australia exports almost all of this shellfish caught in its waters.

Courtesy of Australian Information Service

57

Seen from the thinly wooded Thredbo River Valley, the Snowy Mountains appear thickly clad with trees. As much as 90 percent of Australia's woodlands and forests have been felled or thinned to obtain timber and to clear land for agriculture. In the Snowy Mountains, however, native vegetation has been modified only to a small extent, despite use of the area for hydroelectric power and for recreation.

Photo by Sandi and Jim Provencher

States buy most of the shellfish. Smaller hauls provide whiting, snapper, barramundi, mullet, shark, and mud crabs for local buyers.

Most of Australia's forests, which cover 6 percent of the country's land, blanket the Eastern Highlands and the moist coastal regions. Foresters manage the stands of trees for recreation, for conservation purposes, and for timber production. Most of the native trees are species of gum (eucalyptus). Some types are harvested to produce paper, furniture, and flooring, and others are valued for their gums and oils. Forestry plantations grow crops of pine—especially the Monterey pine from California—for the housing industry. Australia imports—largely from New Zealand—about one-third of the forestry products that it needs.

Courtesy of Australian Information Service

After seasonal rains, rivers that are dry most of the year flow across some roads in the outback. This truck crosses the South Alligator River in the Northern Territory.

Photo by Kay Shaw Photography

A road train, pulling three trailers, moves goods efficiently across the Australian continent. Trucks carry about 80 percent of domestic freight in Australia.

Transportation

About 520,000 miles of roads and 24,000 miles of railways link Australia's cities. Many good highways crisscross the Eastern Highlands from Brisbane southward to Melbourne. Many interior sections of Australia cannot be reached by motor vehicle, however, and no road spans the center of the country from west to east.

Stuart Highway bisects the continent from Darwin in the north to Adelaide in the south. Midway along this route, near the geographic center of Australia, lies Alice Springs. Tourist offices advise people who drive along any road in the outback to make special preparations, because help is not readily available when cars break down in the dry interior.

Qantas Airways, Australia's international air carrier, operates from 10 airports throughout the country. A well-run airline industry is important to the Australian economy. A prolonged strike by pilots on the country's three domestic airlines in 1989 and 1990 discouraged many travelers and hurt many businesses that depended on tourism.

Courtesy of Qantas Airways

The Australian government owns most of the country's railways. The states of New South Wales, Victoria, Queensland, and Western Australia also operate rail systems. Great rivalries existed among these former colonies in the late 1800s when rail lines were put in, and each government adopted tracks of a different gauge. As a result, passengers had to leave one train and board another when crossing colonial boundaries. Mainland capital cities are now connected by standard-gauge track, except for the Adelaide-Melbourne route. Private railways in each state serve mining, industrial, and agricultural areas.

Qantas Airways, the government-run airline, began in the 1920s as a tiny airline serving the outback in Queensland. (Qantas comes from the carrier's original name—Queensland and Northern Territory Aerial Services.) This airline operates from 10 Australian cities. At least 20 other international carriers also serve Australia. The government-owned Trans-Australia Airlines and various private companies offer passenger and freight service within Australia.

Trade

Agricultural and mineral products dominate Australia's export market. Minerals, fuels, and metals earn about half the country's foreign income. Coal is the most important fuel for export purposes, accounting for 15 percent of the country's total foreign earnings. Australia sells crude oil and liquid natural gas on the world market but must import heavy crude oil in order to make some petroleum products. Australia sells more energy resources abroad than it imports.

Agricultural products account for one-third of Australia's exports. Wheat, the country's second highest export earner, brings in about 9 percent of the nation's foreign income. Wool sales earn 6 percent. Japan is Australia's leading customer. In the 1980s, developing countries became in-

A folklift laden with bales of wool backs onto the stern of a ship in Sydney. Australia exports more wool than any other country.

Independent Picture Service

Photo by Emily Slowinski

Unusual animals, such as this wallaby with a joey (baby wallaby) in its pouch, attract visitors to Australia.

Photo by Kay Shaw Photography

Tents shelter campers at Kakadu National Park in the Northern Territory.

creasingly important markets for Australian exporters.

Australia's major imports are vehicles, petroleum and petroleum products, office equipment and computers, industrial machinery, electrical appliances, and textiles. Japan provides most of the vehicle imports, which compete with Australia's own automobile and truck manufacturers. Saudi Arabia and Singapore furnish most of the petroleum imports. Overall, however, the United States is Australia's single largest supplier.

Through its membership in several international trade organizations, Australia seeks to promote trade by working out fair agreements on tariffs and pricing. Under the Closer Economic Relations trade agreement that took effect in 1983, Australia and New Zealand agreed to gradually eliminate all barriers to free trade between them by 1995.

Tourism

Domestic and international tourism is Australia's largest industry. More than one million foreign tourists travel each year to the country, which is particularly appealing for outdoor vacations. Many people go to the beaches of Queensland and scuba dive along the Great Barrier Reef. Inland attractions include Ayers Rock and the Olgas—massive boulders near Alice Springs —as well as winter resorts in the Australian Alps.

Two-thirds of all foreign visitors arrive in Australia via Sydney. The city's harbor, opera house, Harbour Bridge, and surfing at Bondi Beach are among its most popular attractions. During January—when many Australians take their vacations— the city sponsors a month-long festival.

Another stopping point for many foreign vacationers is Melbourne, Australia's second largest city and Sydney's traditional

A scuba diver explores the wonders of the Great Barrier Reef. Water temperatures on the reef are comfortable for divers, who can see thousands of varieties of marine life. Scuba enthusiasts can rent equipment at many island resorts. In addition to diveboats, fishing launches operate from reef islands and from the mainland.

Photo by John Clifton

rival. Although Sydney has overtaken Melbourne as the business and financial heart of the nation, Melburnians claim that their city is still the nation's social and intellectual center. Canberra and the other state capitals are also popular destinations for tourists.

The Future

From its beginnings as a prison colony, Australia developed rapidly into a nation that offered its citizens a high standard of living. Although beset by economic problems in recent years, Australia's future seems bright. The country has a wealth of natural resources and a history of governmental stability. Its unique physical features draw visitors from around the world, and its political steadiness attracts foreign investors.

Although Australia has adapted smoothly to political changes, the society has not been without turmoil. Most disruptions have involved disagreements between industrialists and trade unions. Strikes and the terms of their settlement have seriously hurt the productivity of the economy.

Tension has also surfaced over the rights of Aborigines in a white-dominated society. The Aborigines continue to be a disadvantaged people, and their land claims are still largely unsettled. If Australia's future is to continue on a steady course, the government and the public must find workable solutions to these problems.

Courtesy of Ruth Karl

Australia's mild climate and hundreds of miles of golden beaches encourage tourists to sunbathe, swim, and surf. Every popular beach has a surf-lifesaving club whose members volunteer as lifeguards.

Photo by Sandi and Jim Provencher

The British cruise ship *Queen Mary,* filled with vacationers from Europe, docks in Sydney's harbour.

Index
